SIDESHOWS
&
SPECTACLES

VICTORIAN ENTERTAINMENT

BRITISH LIBRARY

Pomegranate

PORTLAND, OREGON

Pomegranate Communications, Inc.
19018 NE Portal Way, Portland OR 97230
800 227 1428   www.pomegranate.com

Pomegranate Europe Ltd.
'number three', Siskin Drive, Middlemarch Business Park
Coventry CV3 4FJ, UK
+44 (0)24 7621 4461   sales@pomegranate.com

Pomegranate's mission is to invigorate, illuminate, and inspire through art.

Pomegranate publishes books of postcards on a wide range of subjects.
Please contact the publisher for more information.

Front cover: *Mrs. Daffodil Downey's Séance*, c. 1885
Maskelyne & Cooke, Egyptian Hall
The British Library, Evan.397

Back cover: *Mr. Charles Du Val*, 1883
Odds & Ends, St. James's Great Hall
The British Library, Evan.2596

ISBN 978-0-7649-8131-9
Item No. AA1006

Cover designed by Tristen Jackman

Printed in Korea
27 26 25 24 23 22 21 20 19 18   10 9 8 7 6 5 4 3 2 1

To facilitate detachment of the postcards from this book, fold each card along its perforation line before tearing.

HENRY EVANS, a nineteenth-century English conjuror and ventriloquist who performed under the stage name Evanion, was also a lifelong collector of ephemera—posters, handbills, trade cards, catalogs, novelties, and more. He shared this habit with his father (not a performer himself, rather a refreshment seller at popular entertainment venues), collecting printed event materials.

Evanion was a moderately successful performer at the height of his career. An 1866 performance in front of the future King Edward VII and other members of the royal family provided him the moniker "The Royal Conjuror." But he was also a devoted researcher, networking with fellow conjurors and enthusiasts, and spending untold hours at the British Museum investigating the history of his trade.

In need of cash, Evanion sold a great deal of his ephemera collection in 1895 to the British Museum (now in the British Library). Still, his personal collection remained impressive. Nine years later Evanion wrote to Harry Houdini regarding their mutual interests and immediately arranged a meeting, after which the American illusionist dotingly described Evanion's "priceless treasures." The two worked closely together thereafter, until Evanion's death in 1905.

The British Library now owns 5,000 items relating to Victorian entertainment and everyday life in its Evanion Collection.

SIDESHOWS & SPECTACLES

Poole's New Mammoth Diorama, 1882
Royal Victoria Hall
The British Library, Evan.1913

800 227 1428   WWW.POMEGRANATE.COM

Pomegranate

SANGERS' GRAND NATIONAL AMPHITHEATRE

THE THREE GREAT CIRCUS COMPANIES!

LORD MAYORS

SANGER'S

SHOW

and GORGEOUS PANTOMIME entitled,

WHITTINGTON & HIS WONDERFUL CAT

OR HARLEQUIN AND JOHNNY GILPIN AND HIS TRIP TO EDMONTON!

TWO PERFORMANCES DAILY: Afternoons at 2; Evgs. at 7

D. & J. ALLEN, Lithographers & Letterpress Printers, Vine St. South Belfast.

SIDESHOWS & SPECTACLES

Sanger's Lord Mayors Show, 1882
Sanger's Grand National Amphitheatre
The British Library, Evan.2688

800 227 1428   WWW.POMEGRANATE.COM

Pomegranate

SANGER'S AMPHITHEATRE

CIRCUS AND

DOUBLE PANTOMIME

ALADDIN & FORTY THIEVES

JAMES UPTON, BIRMINGHAM.

SIDESHOWS & SPECTACLES

Sanger's Amphitheatre, 1886
Circus and Double Pantomime, Aladdin & Forty Thieves
The British Library, Evan.2590

ALHAMBRA

(WILLIAM HOLLAND) LEICESTER SQUARE. (MANAGER

BABIL AND BIJOU

9 Feet 8 Ft. 7 Ft. 6 Ft. 5 Ft. 4 Ft. 3 Ft. 2 Ft. 1 Foot

GIANT AMAZON QUEEN.

W. SMITH LITHO

SIDESHOWS & SPECTACLES

Babil and Bijou, the Giant Amazon Queen, 1882
Royal Alhambra Theatre
The British Library, Evan.2595

EGYPTIAN HALL

DAILY AT 3 & 8

MODERN WITCHERY

ASTRAL BODY

THE MIRACLE OF LH'ASA.

SIDESHOWS & SPECTACLES

Modern Witchery, 1894
Maskelyne and Cooke, Egyptian Hall
The British Library, Evan.2603

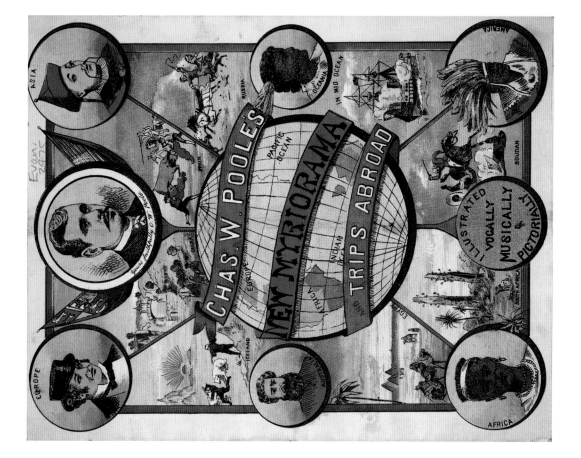

SIDESHOWS & SPECTACLES

Chas W. Poole's New Myriorama and Trips Abroad, n.d.
The British Library, Evan.2475

ALEXANDRA PALACE

DAILY

MYERS'

ELEPHANTS

BATHING

WILLING & KINGS Ltd.

SIDESHOWS & SPECTACLES

Myers' Elephants Bathing, c. 1880
Alexandra Palace
The British Library, Evan.2595a

SIDESHOWS & SPECTACLES

Mr. Charles Du Val, 1883
Odds & Ends, St. James's Great Hall
The British Library, Evan.2596

SANGER'S

AMPHITHEATRE,

CLOSE TO WATERLOO STATION

Lessee and Manager · Mr. CHAS. E. STUART

WHITSUN ATTRACTIONS!

The Great American Drama, entitled

BUFFALO BILL

SPECIAL ENGAGEMENTS

Mr. CHAS. HERMAN   Mr. LIONEL ELLIS

Miss KATE NEVILLE & BUFFALO FRISCO

Surnamed by his Tribe the Firechall of Peace & Vengeance

TREACHEROUS ATTACK ON THE STATE COACH

WILL BE PRODUCED

SATURDAY MAY 28th

FOR TWELVE NIGHTS ONLY.

MORNING PERFORMANCE Whit Monday at 2

POPULAR PRICES.   NO FEES

PHILLIS BROS, Printers. 113, LONDON ROAD, S.E.

SIDESHOWS & SPECTACLES

Buffalo Bill, 1887
Sanger's Amphitheatre
The British Library, Evan.2801

800 227 1428   WWW.POMEGRANATE.COM

Pomegranate

SIDESHOWS & SPECTACLES

Professor Pepper's Ghosts, c. 1885
Royal Polytechnic Institution
The British Library, Evan.446

COLE'S NEW PROGRAMME!

BRIXTON HALL, ACRE LANE.

FRIDAY, SATURDAY & MONDAY, OCT. 17, 18 & 20, 1890.

GRAND MORNING PERFORMANCE SATURDAY, OCT. 18th, at 2.30 for 3.

Numbered Stalls, 3s.   Reserved Chairs, 2s.   Unreserved, 1s.   Gallery, 6d.

Children and Schools Half-price to Morning Performance only.   Doors Open, Evening, 7.30 for 8; Saturday Morning, 2.30 for 3.

Carriages: Morning at 4.30½; Evening at 10.   Tickets at Druxaire's Pianoforte Warehouse, Acre Lane, Brixton; J. Fearon, Post Office, 304, Brixton Road; Smith's Library, Railton Road, Brixton; and of Hall Keeper.

COLE'S REVIVED COMIC CONCERT PARTY

ASSISTED BY

MR. ARTHUR W. RIGBY
VOCALIST, COMEDIAN, AND MIMIC, A LA MR. GEO. GROSSMITH, LATE OF THE CRYSTAL PALACE, SYDENHAM.

MISS KATIE NANTON
THE CHARMING SOUBRETTE AND VOCALIST.

MR. WALTER PASSMORE
THE WELL-KNOWN ECCENTRIC VOCAL COMEDIAN AND MIMIC.

MADAME SESOR'S

LITTLE BLACK PEARLS
A WONDER OF MECHANICAL SKILL, LATE OF THE CRYSTAL PALACE, SYDENHAM.

MR. VIVIAN BLANCHARD
BUFFO VOCALIST, SOLO PIANIST, &c.

ALLY SLOPER & HERR STINGYMAN
THE ORIGINAL M.P. FOR SHOE LANE, F.O.M. &c.   WHO WILL EXHIBIT HIS ELECTRIC FEATURES.

LIEUT. WALTER COLE
THE HIGHLY POPULAR AND GIFTED VENTRILOQUIST, AND LEADING HUMOURIST AND MIMIC OF THE DAY,
IN A NEW ENTERTAINMENT WITH HIS WONDERFUL ELECTRIC FIGURES.

The Combined Performances of the above Artistes will constitute an Entertainment and Concert of the most Amusing and thoroughly Refined Character, replete with Sparkling Music, Superb Costumes, &c.

THE PLATFORM WILL BE ELEGANTLY FURNISHED
BY THOS. WALLIS & CO., HOLBORN.

Sole Proprietor   -   LIEUT. WALTER COLE, Portland Lodge, Holland Road, Brixton, London, S.W.
Advance Agent   -   Mr. FENTON WALSH   Bill Inspector   Mr. H. VICK.

☞ SEE OTHER BILLS. ☜

STAFFORD & CO., PRINTERS, NETHERFIELD, NEAR NOTTINGHAM.

SIDESHOWS & SPECTACLES

Walter Cole's Refined Comic Concert Party, 1890
Brixton Hall
The British Library, Evan.2814

Pomegranate

800 227 1428   WWW.POMEGRANATE.COM

SIDESHOWS & SPECTACLES

Poole's Grand Pictorial Tours, 1885
Royal Victoria Hall
The British Library, Evan.1899

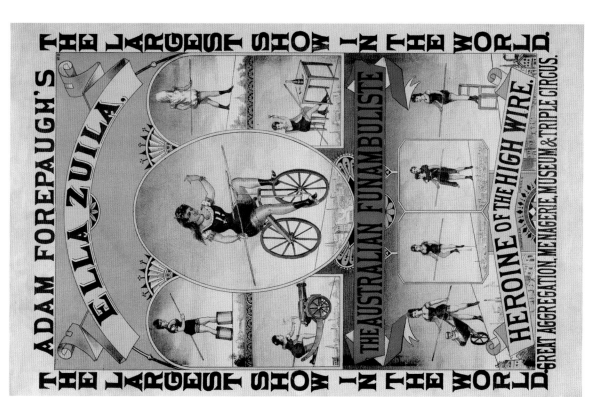

ADAM FOREPAUGH'S THE LARGEST SHOW IN THE WORLD.

ELLA ZUILA.

THE AUSTRALIAN FUNAMBULISTE

HEROINE OF THE HIGH WIRE.

GREAT AGGREGATION, MENAGERIE, MUSEUM & TRIPLE CIRCUS.

THE LARGEST SHOW IN THE WORLD.

SIDESHOWS & SPECTACLES

Ella Zuila, 1885
The Australian Funambuliste
The British Library, Evan.373

800 227 1428   WWW.POMEGRANATE.COM

Pomegranate

EGYPTIAN HALL, PICCADILLY,

EVERY EVENING AT 8 SATURDAY MORNINGS AT 3.

MR. FLEMING NORTON,

*S

ZACHARIAH CHUCKLEHEAD,

IN HIS

MUSICAL & MIMETIC ENTERTAINMENT,

ENTITLED

MR. PERKINS'S PIC-NIC.

SIDESHOWS & SPECTACLES

Mr. Fleming Norton at Egyptian Hall, 1873
Zachariah Chucklehead
The British Library, Evan.2752

800 227 1428 WWW.POMEGRANATE.COM

Pomegranate

AGRICULTURAL HALL
WORLD'S FAIR

LESSEES.. H.&T. READ & F. BAILEY.

THIS ENTERTAINMENT FREE OF CHARGE

RICHARDSON'S SHOW · PERFORMING DOGS · WAX WORKS · MARIONETTES

MOREY'S · TIGERS · PERFORMING LION

OPEN DEC.R 23RD AND 5 FOLLOWING WEEKS

ACCOMMODATION FOR 100,000 People. WET or DRY

ADMISSION SIXPENCE

NO EXTRA CHARGE FOR THE MENAGERIE.

SIDESHOWS & SPECTACLES

World's Fair, 1874
Royal Agricultural Hall
The British Library, Evan.442

800 227 1428 WWW.POMEGRANATE.COM

Pomegranate

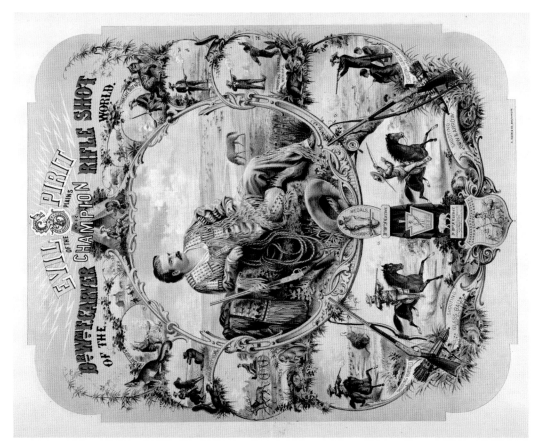

SIDESHOWS & SPECTACLES

Evil Spirit of the Plains, c. 1880
Dr. William Carver
The British Library, Evan.189

SIDESHOWS & SPECTACLES

Beauty and the Beast, 1890
Augustus Harris' Pantomime, Theatre Royal Drury Lane
The British Library, Evan.196

800 227 1428   WWW.POMEGRANATE.COM

Pomegranate

PRINCESS'S ✛ THEATRE.

HANDS-ACROSS-THE-SEA.
BY HENRY PETTITT.

A REPRIEVE! A REPRIEVE! — MILLER & ELLISTON'S COMBINATION

Thursday, November 8th, & Every Evening.

SIDESHOWS & SPECTACLES

Hands Across the Sea, 1888
Miller & Elliston, Princess's Theatre
The British Library, Evan.236

CRIMES of PARIS

OLYMPIC THEATRE
EVERY EVENING

CLEMENT-SMITH & Cº. LONDON

SIDESHOWS & SPECTACLES

Crimes of Paris, c. 1883
Olympic Theatre
The British Library, Evan.237

MANHOOD

Commencing Monday, July 7th. ELEPHANT & CASTLE THEATRE For SIX Nights

SIDESHOWS & SPECTACLES

Manhood, c. 1890
Elephant & Castle Theatre
The British Library, Evan.248

800 227 1428 WWW.POMEGRANATE.COM

Pomegranate

ST. GEORGE'S OPERA HOUSE,
LANGHAM PLACE, OXFORD CIRCUS.

ENCORES NIGHTLY.

ROARS OF LAUGHTER.

(SCENE FROM THE)

STANNARD & DIXON, IMP.7 POLAND ST OXFORD ST.

CONTRABANDISTA.
EVERY EVENING AT ½ PAST 7.
MORNING PERFORMANCE EVERY FRIDAY AT 2.

ADMISSION.
PIT 1/- BALCONY 2/-
STALLS 3/- ORCHESTRA STALLS 5/-

ADMISSION.
PIT 1/- BALCONY 2/-
STALLS 3/- ORCHESTRA STALLS 5/-

SIDESHOWS & SPECTACLES

Contrabandista, c. 1868
St. George's Opera House
The British Library, Evan.440

800 227 1428   WWW.POMEGRANATE.COM

Pomegranate

SIDESHOWS & SPECTACLES

Herr Winkelmeier, 1887
London Pavilion
The British Library, Evan.254

800 227 1428   WWW.POMEGRANATE.COM

Pomegranate

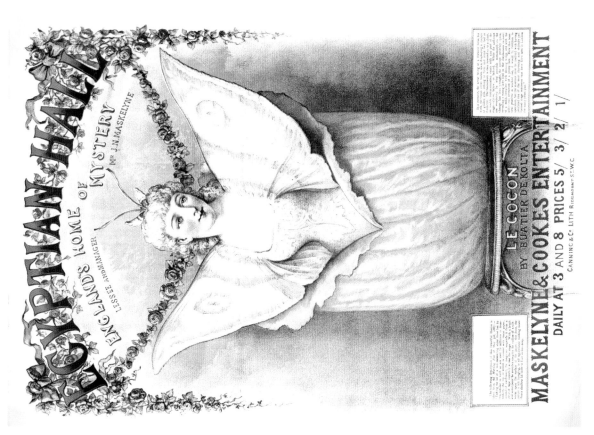

EGYPTIAN HALL

ENGLAND'S HOME OF MYSTERY

LESSEE AND MANAGER Mr J.N.MASKELYNE

LE COCON
BY BUATIER DE KOLTA

MASKELYNE & COOKES ENTERTAINMENT

DAILY AT 3 AND 8   PRICES 5/ 3/ 2/ 1/

CANNINC & Cº LITH RIDGMONT ST W C

SIDESHOWS & SPECTACLES

The Cocoon Illusion, 1887
Buatier De Kolta, Egyptian Hall
The British Library, Evan.330

800 227 1428   WWW.POMEGRANATE.COM

Pomegranate

EGYPTIAN HALL.

MASKELYNE & COOKE'S ENTERTAINMENT.

MRS. DAFFODIL DOWNEY'S SEANCE,

INCLUDING Mr. MASKELYNE'S RECENTLY ADDED

MARVELLOUS ILLUSIONS !

EVERY EVENING AT EIGHT & TUESDAY, THURSDAY & SATURDAY AFTERNOONS AT THREE.

FOR FURTHER PARTICULARS SEE DAILY PAPERS

STAFFORD & CO., Printers, Netherfield, near Nottingham.

SIDESHOWS & SPECTACLES

Mrs. Daffodil Downey's Séance, c. 1885
Maskelyne & Cooke, Egyptian Hall
The British Library, Evan.397

SIDESHOWS & SPECTACLES

The Fakirs of Benares, 1884
Maskelyne and Cooke, Egyptian Hall
The British Library, Evan.404

EGYPTIAN HALL.

ENGLAND'S HOME OF MYSTERY.

UNDER THE MANAGEMENT OF MR W. MORTON.

MASKELYNE AND COOKE

TEMPTATIONS OF GOOD S^T ANTHONY.

MR MASKELYNE'S NEW ILLUSORY SKETCH

A PERFORMANCE EVERY DAY, (SEE NEWSPAPER ADVERTISEMENTS)
WHETHER AFTERNOON OR EVENING.)

Clement Smith & Co^y Grenville Steam Works, Star Yard, Lane, St Clement's Lane, London

SIDESHOWS & SPECTACLES

Temptations of Good St. Anthony, 1881
Maskelyne and Cooke, Egyptian Hall
The British Library, Evan.410

800 227 1428 WWW.POMEGRANATE.COM

Pomegranate

GREATEST COMPANY IN THE WORLD, THE MOST WONDERFUL RIDERS, GYMNASTS, ACROBATS & COMICAL CLOWNS EXTANT.

TWO PERFORMANCES DAILY, AFTERNOON AT 2, EVENING AT 7.

THE GORGEOUS SCENE OF BLUE BEARD'S PALACE & GARDENS.

SANGERS HIPPODROME, CIRCUS & MENAGERIE GRAND PANTOMIME BLUE BEARD, 20 ELEPHANTS, DROMEDARIES &c.

PATRONIZED BY HIS ROYAL HIGHNESS THE PRINCE OF WALES & ROYAL FAMILY.   PERFORMANCES, AFTERNOON AT TWO, EVENING AT SEVEN.

SIDESHOWS & SPECTACLES

Circus and Menagerie, c. 1881
Sanger's Hippodrome
The British Library, Evan.415

EGYPTIAN HALL.
MASKELYNE & COOKE.
ILLUSTRATION OF THE NEW FEATURE.

TO THE AFFLICTED
DR. DE BOLUS'S
ELIXIR
VITÆ!
N.B. NO PUFFING REQUIRED.

COMIC ILLUSORY SKETCH, ELIXIR VITÆ,
In which Mr. Maskelyne performs the astounding and amusing feat of taking off Mr. Cooke's Head.   All London is going to see it.

EVERY EVENING at 8, also on Tuesday, Thursday, and Saturday Afternoons at 3.

W. Morton, Manager.

ADMISSION 1/- 2/- 3/- & 5/-

RAYNER & CARPENTER, STEAM PRINTERS, 7, BELLE COURT, LUDGATE CIRCUS, E.C., & GRAVESEND.

SIDESHOWS & SPECTACLES

Comic Illusory Sketch, Elixir Vitæ, 1878
Maskelyne & Cooke, Egyptian Hall
The British Library, Evan.431

SIDESHOWS & SPECTACLES

Henry & Walter Wardroper, the Twin-Like Mimics, 1873
Messrs. Hunt & Sparrow, Town Hall
The British Library, Evan.508

800 227 1428   WWW.POMEGRANATE.COM

Pomegranate

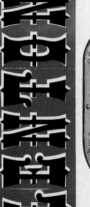

SIDESHOWS & SPECTACLES

Lenton Family, c. 1886
South London Palace
The British Library, Evan.9014

800 227 1428   WWW.POMEGRANATE.COM

Pomegranate